The Yellow Wall-Paper Sanity Journal

what to do in your own four walls

sara barkat & sonia barkat

ts T. S. Poetry Press • New York

T. S. Poetry Press
Ossining, New York
Tspoetry.com

Cover images by Sara Barkat

ISBN 978-1-943120-46-8

The Yellow Wall-Paper Sanity Journal:
   What to Do in Your Own Four Walls

      Author & Illustrator, Sara Barkat
      Author, Sonia Barkat
      ISBN 978-1-943120-46-8

Illustrations first appeared in *The Yellow Wall-Paper: A Graphic Novel*, by Charlotte Perkins Gilman, illustrated by Sara Barkat, and are used with permission of T. S. Poetry Press.

"VaudeVillanelle," by David K. Wheeler, first appeared at *Tweetspeak Poetry* and is used with permission of T. S. Poetry Press.

"Migration," by Sara Barkat, first appeared in *Every Day Poems* and is used with permission of the poet.

Kerfuffle limerick first appeared at *Tweetspeak Poetry* and is used with permission of T. S. Poetry Press.

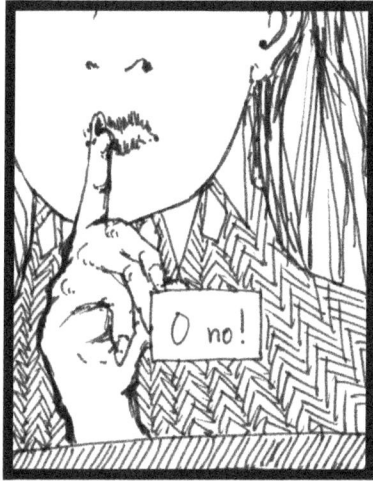

inspired by

The Yellow Wall-Paper

graphic novel

count the number of walls in your house

_____ walls

where are they? (where shouldn't they be?)

**what is the last thing you'd want
to look at for the rest of your life?**

draw it in the room below

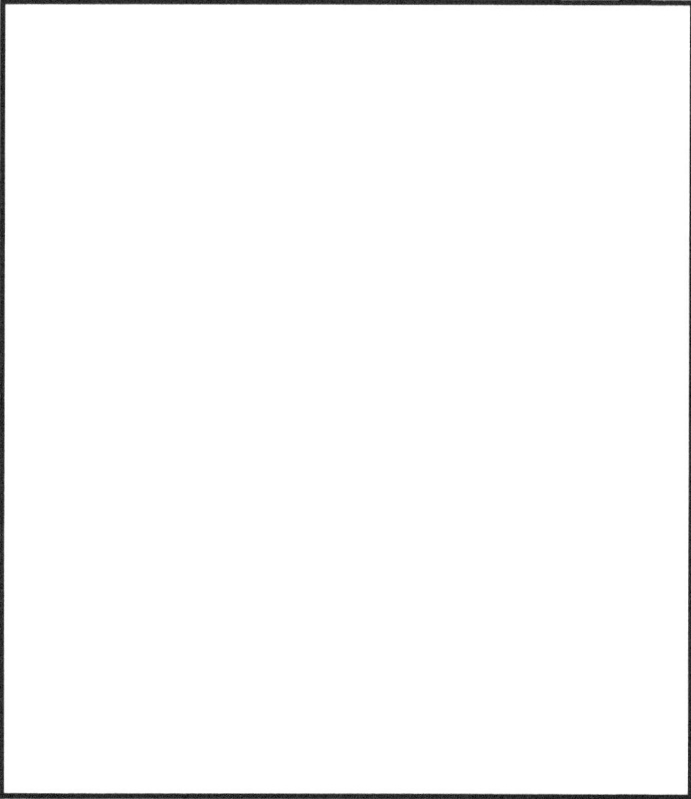

turn the page so it can't get out

what stars do you see in the sky tonight?

befriend them

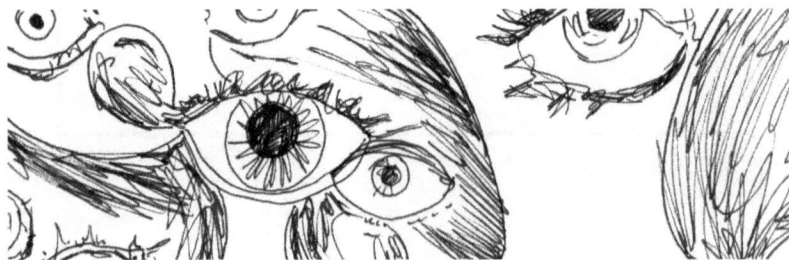

(they'll be watching you fall asleep)

**what is your least favorite color?
wear it today. record the experience**

_____

_____

_____

_____

_____

_____

_____

_____

_____

_____

_____

write a free verse poem

incorporate the prompted line

_____

_____

_____

_____

_____

_____

_____

_____

_____

— but that would be asking too much of fate!
_____

draw your hand

what are you holding?

why?

why not?

write a catalogue poem
about the objects sitting next to you right now

repeated
word/phrase:

beginning or end of line?
you choose!

The Steps to Write a Catalogue Poem Are Simple

1. Repeat a single word or phrase at the beginning of your lines

2. Repeat a single word or phrase at the end of your lines

3. Mix it up. When it starts to feel boring, stop cataloging for a few lines

example from "On Restlessness"…

There was never a time that I knew everything.
There wasn't a night I wanted you to lose sleep.
There are some words you can say with a blink.
There are nights I wake up curled on the floor.
There are appliances that refuse to operate.
There are solutions that don't have a question.

—David K. Wheeler

for more on how to write a catalogue poem,
visit tweetspeak poetry at:

https://www.tweetspeakpoetry.com/2011/05/21/
how-to-write-a-catalog-poem-or-not/

use chalk to make
your sidewalk
yellow

cover your furniture with sheets

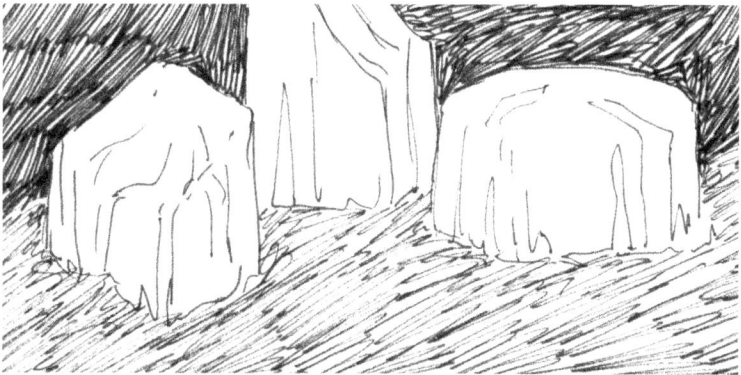

write a free verse poem using the phrases below

sprawl

outrageous angles

artistic sin

little distance

provoke

describe your room

in moonlight

in twilight

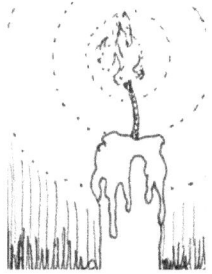

in candlelight

in lamplight

what you say

what you think

do you like your room?

critique.

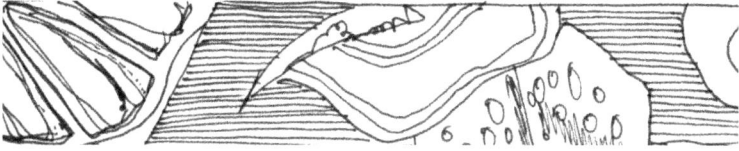

things that are a
nice shade of
yellow

things that are a
nasty shade of
yellow

what's this?
it tells you when
the end words of
the poem should
have the same
rhymes

like snake & bake!

write a pantoum about
yellow things!

for ideas, look at your list of
nice & nasty things (on the
previous page)

A

_____ 1

B

_____ 2

A

_____ 3

B

_____ 4

keep
rhyming
alternat-
ing
lines!

_____ 2

_____ 5

_____ 3

_____ 6

this is just numbering the lines of the poem so it's easier to refer to them. why? because in a pantoum, you repeat lines a lot!

so when the numbers "1" & "2" show up again, you know that means... copy down the line again just like before :)

_____ 5

_____ 7

_____ 6

_____ 8

_____ 7

_____ 9

_____ 8

_____ 10

... just add as many more stanzas as you like! then when you want to, finish the poem:

_____ 9

_____ 3

_____ 10

_____ 1

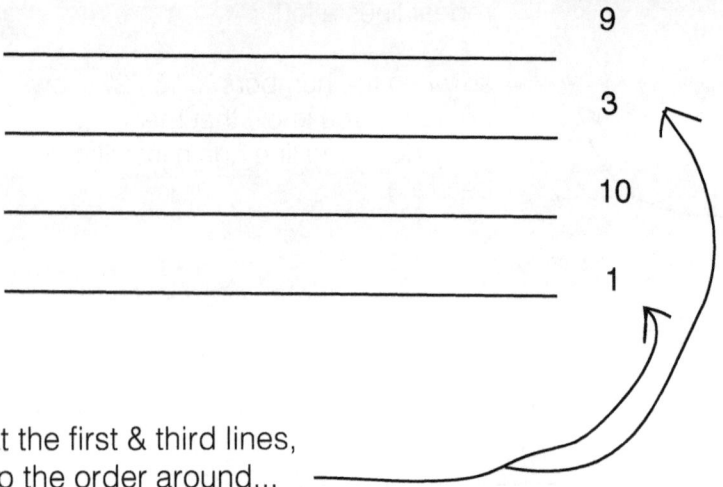

repeat the first & third lines,
but flip the order around...

so your poem ends with the
same line it started with!

for more information on pantoums,
you can go to tweetspeak poetry:

https://www.tweetspeakpoetry.com/2013/
03/04/5-great-ways-to-write-a-pantoum/

extra space
to write, if
you need it

if you don't need
the space to write,
scribble pictures!

(this pantoum is getting longer than the wallpaper!)

escape!

START

END

what creeps?

_____ creeps.

_____ creeps.

_____ creeps.

_____ creeps.

_____ creeps.

_____ creeps.

_____ creeps.

_____ creeps.

_____ creeps.

_____ creeps.

_____ creeps.

write down the last dream you can remember

eat blackberries

climb up the walls

write a poem about things that creep

unblinking

splintered

add these words, if you like

impertinence

everlastingness

sideways

crawl

wink

ravage

draw a toadstool

draw a toad sitting on it

give the toad a friend

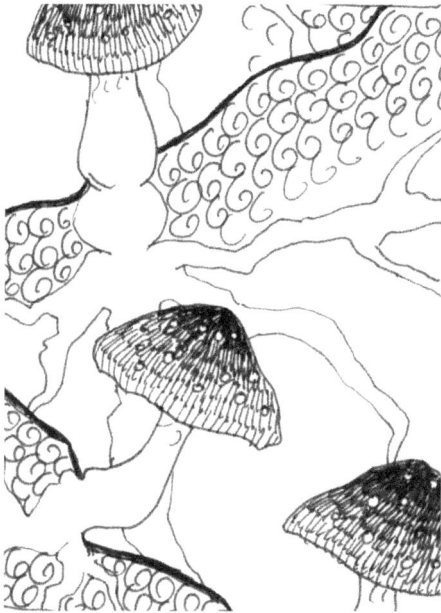

be a hermit for a day

(hermits don't have wi-fi)

walk in circles until
you get dizzy

**turn to a random page in this journal,
that you've filled out already**

use the words and pictures on that page
to inspire a villanelle

what's a villanelle?

A   _____ 1

B   _____ 2

A   _____ 3

↙

etc!

_____

_____

_____ 1

_____

_____

_____ 3

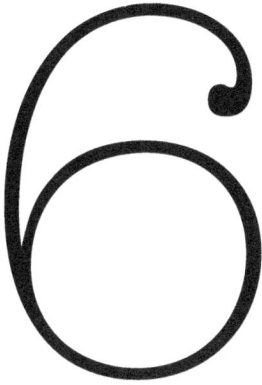

6 stanzas

_____

_____

_____ 1

_____

_____

_____ 3

A _____

B _____

A _____ 1

A _____ 3

one example

VaudeVillanelle

Kick and dance onto the stage—
as the piano man bangs a ditty—
rush behind the theater drapes

Do you enjoy the wild old cabaret?
Do you like how the young ladies
kick and dance onto the stage?

But don't blush or try saving face
while you watch our brand of comedy
rush behind the theater drapes

because champing right at its tail
a new bit or gag, and something witty
kick and dance onto the stage.

Lacing dialog in the one-act play
the satire will get a mite snippy,
rush behind the theater drapes,

and tweak it up with shadow shapes.
Then comes the closing routine:
kick and dance onto the stage,
rush behind the theater drapes.

—David K. Wheeler

Migration

Words have roots unlike trees do
they are sideways and insubstantial
moving blackbird wings flew

Casting arrows flame-blue
burning bracken crackle-fall
words have roots unlike trees do

A wisp, a whisper, willow grew
passing figments figures tall
moving blackbird wings flew

They of all the birds knew
how words inseparable yet had parts
words have roots unlike trees do

For trees have rings but words undo
the trees from rings and roots from hearts
moving black, bird-wings flew

Over bright span of all we view
the snaking draw and fluting crawl
for words have roots unlike trees do
and move like blackbirds' wings flew.

— Sara Barkat

for more about how to write a villanelle,
check out tweetspeak poetry:

https://www.tweetspeakpoetry.com/2011/12/02/i-see-
you-in-there-the-villanelle/

"I always fancy I see people walking in these numerous paths and arbors"

look out your window. make up stories about the people passing by

if you see no people, look harder

design a perfume that smells like yellow

notes:

_____

_____

_____

_____

_____

_____

_____

_____

_____

_____

_____

_____

_____

_____

_____

when you're isolated somewhere,
nothing keeps a calendar except nature . . .

mon.	tues.	wed.	thur.

**press a flower or plant for each day
of the month**

fri.	*sat.*	*sun.*

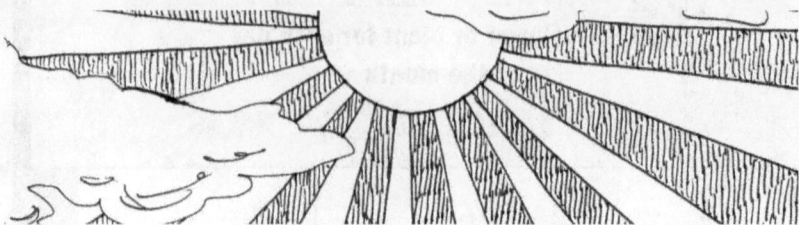

trace the shadows of clouds

"I have watched her sometimes away off in the open country,

creeping as fast as a cloud shadow in a high wind."

**go to a
garden**

transcribe a mundane dialogue

give it ominous import

go horseback riding.

if this is not possible, build a horse to ride

find the loneliest wall in your house.

keep it company

go somewhere abandoned.

pen some lore on how it got that way

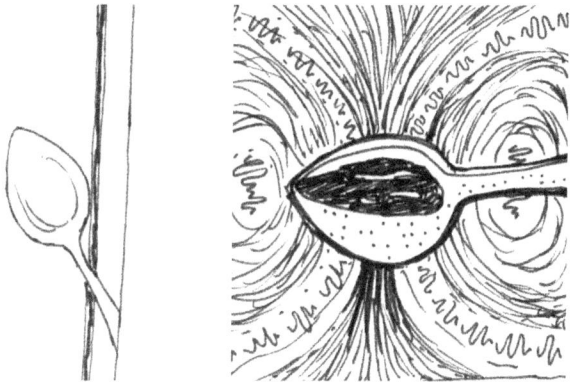

cod liver oil is so last year.
start your day with a spoonful of olive oil

leave the spoons in a row for a week

write about a journey.

incorporate some of the phrases below

crosslights fade

(headlong plunge)

(a room for worlds)

where are you going?

why?

open all the windows. see what it's like
outside

take a bath

let your thoughts float

hide your writing in unlikely places

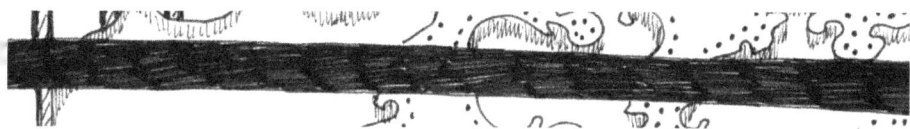

a place for phrases you hear

why are they notable?

do you like them?

dislike them?

**write a vilanelle with some of
your phrases**

(you met the villanelle
about 20 pages ago)

get out. at last

(what were you in?)

talk to the person living in your wall.

what can they tell you that you don't already know?

write your sorrows on a page

let them fade in the sun

stand barefoot outside. it's not fair to
keep walking all over your shoes

find a path to run on

"I cry at nothing, and cry most of the time"

cry about nothing

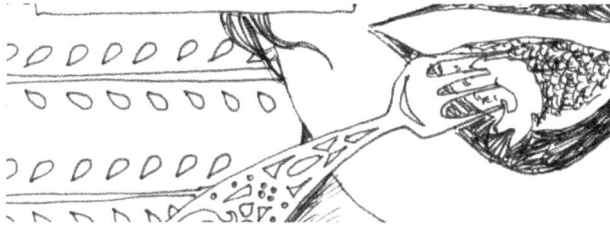

eat a meal you don't like.

write about the experience.

paint your nails yellow

scratch off the polish

find the most melodramatic way to lie on your bed

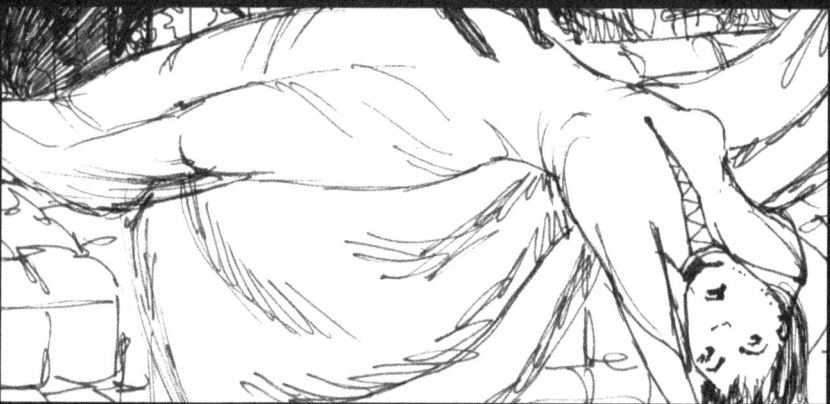

write another pantoum (they're moody)

turn to a random part of your journal
for inspiration

cont. $\longrightarrow$

haunt your house in the dark

creep about

catalogue species of roses

"I will take a nap I guess."

write about how tired you are

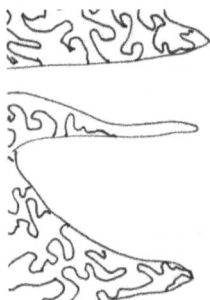

• take a nap

make yourself popcorn.

watch the furniture.

it makes the best entertainment

(phones on silent. don't let anything disrupt the show)

write a scary poem with these words

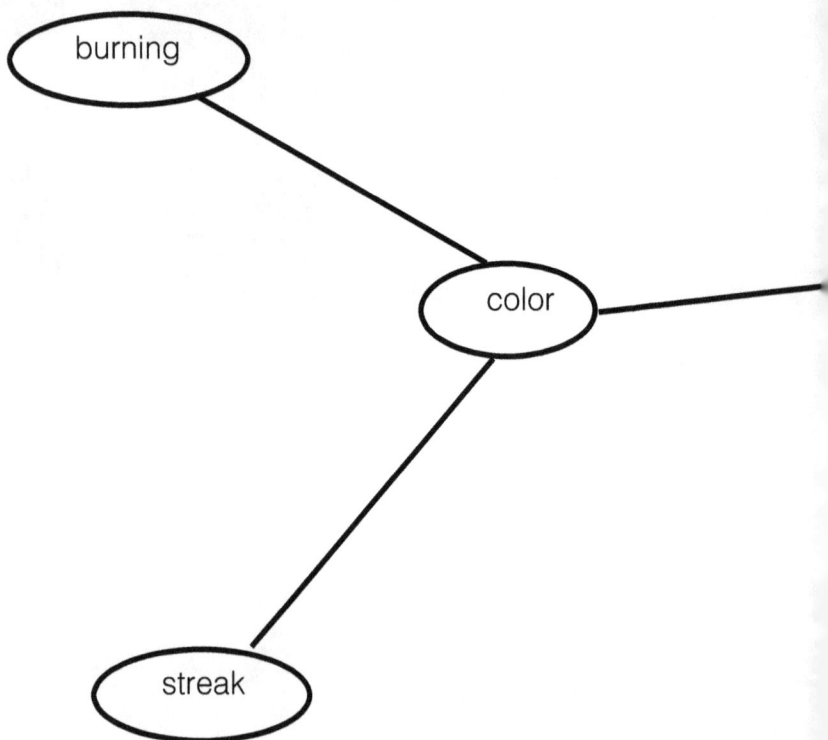

burning

color

streak

rubbed

gentle

peculiar

can you write a funny poem
with the same words?

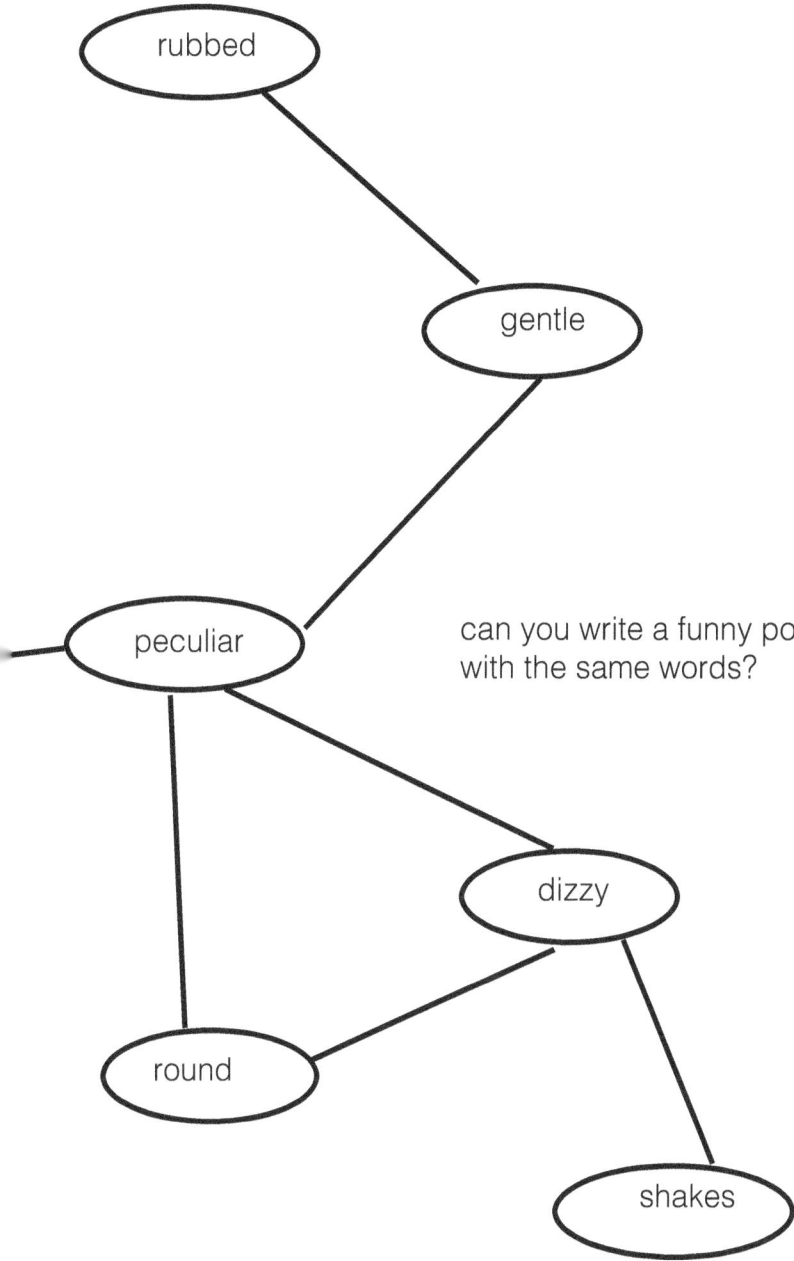

dizzy

round

shakes

did you watch the furniture?

good!

**write a limerick about
the experience**

A _____

A _____

B _____

B _____

A _____

begin a kerfuffle with your limerick

The limerick's an interesting form
They say that *offense* is really the norm
If some feathers aren't ruffled
Or you've begun no kerfuffle
Your poem is sure to underperform.

—Will Willingham

limericks are written in anapestic meter
(each foot has two short and one long syllable).
creep over to to tweetspeak poetry for a refresh...

https://www.tweetspeakpoetry.com/2017/04/06/how-
to-write-a-limerick-infographic/

open your window in the morning.

read a poem to the birds

sing your bedroom wall a lullabye
before you fall asleep

An Unconvincing Poem

_____ dear

danger _____

_____ could

_____ would

flesh _____

_____ hours

who does the poem belong to?

draw what's hiding behind it

put googly eyes on your furniture,

so it can keep an eye on you

turn off the light.

shine a flashlight on your walls.

make shadows

draw your nightmare

why is it frightening?

draw a key

what is it for?

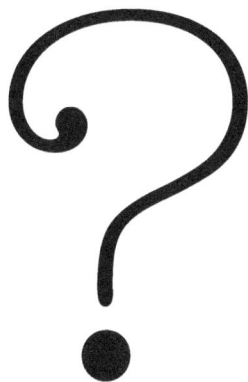

write a poem using these words

stained

innocent

smell

yellow

smooches

touched

draw wallpaper on this page.

stick it on a wall.

add more pages till it drives you crazy

tear it all down

The End

or

is it

the

beginning?

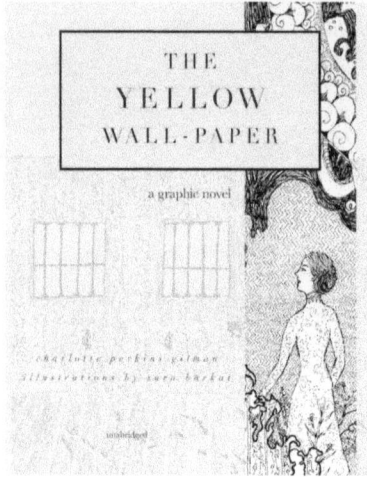

where it all began

(the yellow wall-paper: a graphic novel—
full text by charlotte perkins gilman, 1892
illustrations by sara barkat, 2020)

www.ingramcontent.com/pod-product-compliance
Lightning Source LLC
Chambersburg PA
CBHW021935040426
42448CB00008B/1071